HEALTHY BODY

Exercise and Your Body

Polly Goodman

HODDER
Wayland

an imprint of Hodder Children's Books

This book is based on the original title *How Does Exercise Affect Me?* by Judy Sadgrove, in the *Health and Fitness* series, published in 1999 by Hodder Wayland

This differentiated text edition is written by Polly Goodman and published in Great Britain in 2005 by Hodder Wayland, an imprint of Hodder Children's Books.

Editor: Kirsty Hamilton
Designer: Jane Hawkins
Consultant: Jayne Wright

Picture acknowledgements:
Digital Vision 6, 8, 16, 17, 36, 38 top, 40 top; Image Bank 43 top (Marc Romaneli); Science Photo Library 18 top (BSIP Vem), 21 (Scott Camazine), 35 (Biophoto), 44 (Oscar Burriel/Latin Stock); Tony Stone Images 1 (Terry Vine), 5 (David Young Wolff), 7 (Lori Adamski Peek), 12 (Bruce Ayres), 13 (Amwell), 14 (Amwell), 15 (Dave Rosenberg), 19 (Ian O'Leary), 20 (Bill Robbins), 22 (James Darrell), 23 (Al Bello), 24 (Bob Torrez), 25 (Penny Tweedie), 26 (Amwell), 28 (Bill Truslow), 31 (Bruce Ayres), 37 (Robert Aschenbrenner), 38 bottom (Terry Vine), 40 bottom (John McDermott), 42 (Bob Torrez), 45 top (Bruce Ayres), 45 bottom (David Madison); John Walmsley Photography 4, 10, 27, 29, 30-31, 34; Hodder Wayland Picture Library 18 bottom. The artwork on page 9 is by Peter Bull. The artwork on page 11 is by Alex Pang. The artwork on pages 32-33 is by Michael Posen.

All possible care has been taken to trace the ownership of each photograph and to obtain permission for its use. If there are any omissions or if any errors have occurred, they will be corrected in subsequent editions, on notification to the publisher.

British Library Cataloguing in Publication Data
Goodman, Polly
Exercise and your body. - Differentiated ed. - (Healthy body)
1. Exercise - Juvenile literature
I. Title
613.7'1

ISBN 0 7502 47177

Printed in China

Hodder Children's Books
A division of Hodder Headline Limited
338 Euston Road, London NW1 3BH

Contents

Why do We Need Exercise?

Our bodies were designed to be on the move. Long ago, people walked around for most of each day, looking for food. Nowadays, we spend most of the time sitting down, travelling in buses or cars, at our desks at work or school, or watching television at home. This inactive lifestyle is bad for our health.

Like any machine that isn't used for a while, our bodies don't work as well if we're not using them regularly. When we don't do any exercise, our bodies lose fitness. When we are unfit, our heart, lungs, blood, bones and muscles do not work as well. People who are extremely unfit are more likely to have heart attacks and other diseases. They are also more likely to be overweight.

Taking exercise does not just make our bodies work better. It makes us feel and look better. Exercise keeps us slimmer, gives us more energy, and it's fun! You don't have to be good at sport to take exercise. Any kind of activity that involves movement is exercise, whether it's table tennis or football, skateboarding, or simply walking.

We can keep a basic level of fitness by making sure we take enough exercise. But if we want to make our bodies perform at their best, we have to train them with special exercises.

Basketball helps to build up bones and strengthen leg muscles. ▶

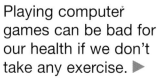

Playing computer games can be bad for our health if we don't take any exercise. ▶

What is Fitness?

Physical fitness is made up of three different things: aerobic fitness, muscular fitness, and flexibility. Our bodies need to have all three to be physically fit.

Aerobic fitness is the ability to keep doing an activity that makes us breathless, such as running, cycling or brisk walking. These are all types of aerobic exercise. To improve our aerobic fitness, we have to take more aerobic exercise.

Aerobic exercise

Aerobic exercise makes the heart and lungs work harder. It uses oxygen that we breathe in through our lungs to release energy from our body fat. ('Aerobic' means 'with oxygen'.)

Swimming is good aerobic exercise because it makes the heart and lungs work hard. ▼

Benefits of aerobic exercise

Aerobic exercise is good for the heart. By making the heart work harder, regular aerobic exercise makes the heart strong and fit. People with a fit heart are less likely to get heart disease.

Aerobic exercise can also help us keep slim. When we breathe a lot of oxygen, the fat stored in our bodies is burnt and used as energy. So taking aerobic exercise can stop us getting overweight, or help us lose any unwanted fat.

Step classes are a fun way to improve aerobic fitness with other people. ▶

Breathing

When we breathe in, our lungs take in oxygen and pass it to the blood. The heart pumps the blood to the heart, and then to our legs and other parts of our body. Our muscles use the oxygen to make energy, and dump carbon dioxide back into the blood. This blood returns to the heart and back to the lungs. The carbon dioxide is released when we breathe out.

When we take aerobic exercise, we breathe more quickly and our heart beats faster to get more oxygen around our bodies.

▲ Speed cycling is an intensive form of aerobic exercise because it makes the heart and lungs work very hard.

Types of aerobic exercise

- Brisk walking
- Running
- Swimming
- Aerobics classes
- Cycling
- Rowing
- Dancing
- Exercise machines
- Football and other team sports

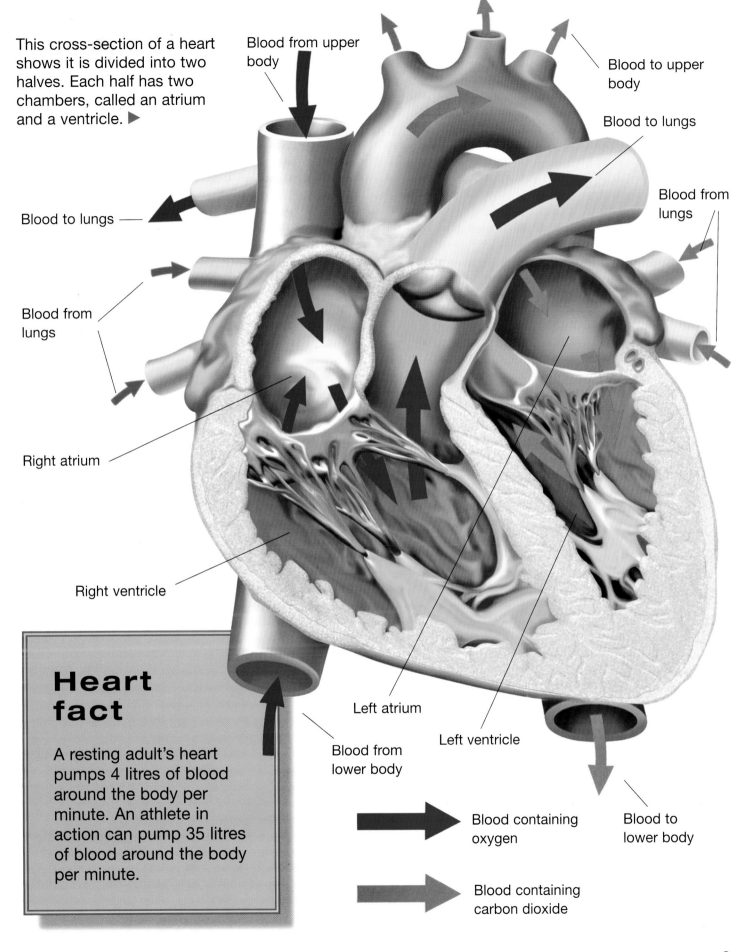

This cross-section of a heart shows it is divided into two halves. Each half has two chambers, called an atrium and a ventricle. ▶

Blood from upper body

Blood to upper body

Blood to lungs

Blood to lungs

Blood from lungs

Blood from lungs

Right atrium

Right ventricle

Left atrium

Left ventricle

Blood from lower body

Blood to lower body

Blood containing oxygen

Blood containing carbon dioxide

Heart fact

A resting adult's heart pumps 4 litres of blood around the body per minute. An athlete in action can pump 35 litres of blood around the body per minute.

9

Types of anaerobic exercise

- Weight lifting
- Weight machines
- Press-ups and other floor exercises
- Toning classes
- Sprinting and jumping

Muscular fitness

Muscular fitness is the strength of muscles and their ability to keep working. It is the ability to lift weight and produce force quickly. Weightlifting, sprinting and jumping all require muscular fitness.

We can improve our muscular fitness by putting pressure against our muscles. Exercises such as lifting weights do this. This type of exercise is called anaerobic, or 'without oxygen' exercise because the main energy it uses is not produced using oxygen. Instead, anaerobic exercise uses energy from glycogen, a carbohydrate stored in the muscles.

Arm bends

Triceps muscle relaxes and lengthens.

◀ Using weight machines in the gym improves anaerobic fitness by putting pressure against them.

Triceps muscle pulls and shortens, straightening the arm at the elbow.

Biceps muscle pulls and shortens, bending the arm at the elbow.

Forearm bends.

How muscles work

There are about 600 muscles in the human body. They support our skeleton and allow us to move by pulling our joints. Muscles work in pairs. When one muscle pulls, the other relaxes. When you bend your arm at the elbow, the biceps at the front of the arm pull and shorten, while the triceps at the back of the arm relax and lengthen (see diagram). When you straighten your arm the opposite happens. The triceps pull and shorten, while the biceps relax and lengthen.

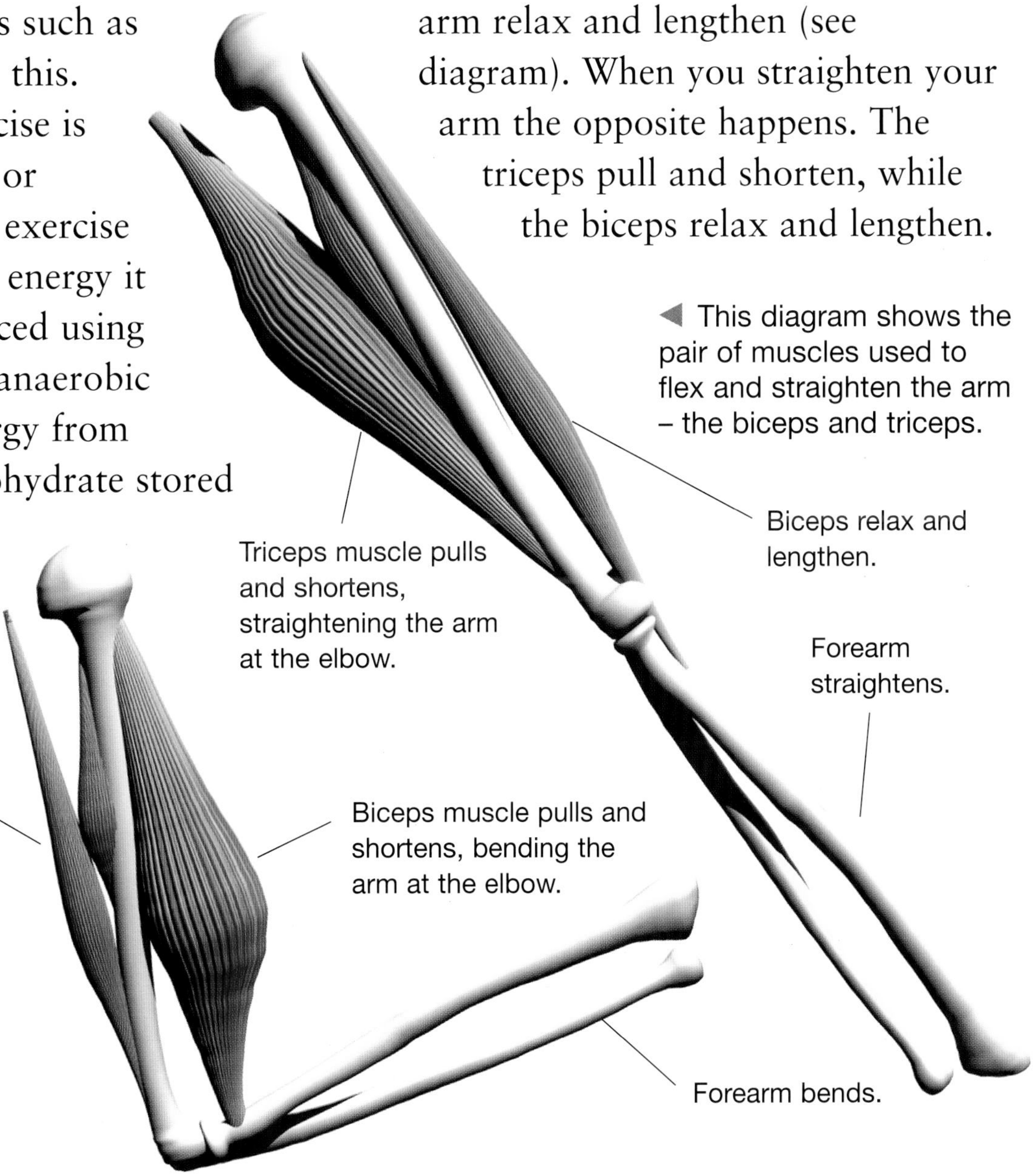

◀ This diagram shows the pair of muscles used to flex and straighten the arm – the biceps and triceps.

Biceps relax and lengthen.

Forearm straightens.

A sports doctor checks an athlete's leg. Muscular fitness reduces the chance of accidental injury. ▼

Weight lifters can lift up to five times their body weight. ▶

Weights

Never lift heavy weights if you are under 18 because you are still growing and it may damage your bones. Instead, do lots of repetitions with lighter weights.

Benefits of muscular fitness

People with muscular fitness are stronger. This means that everyday tasks, such as carrying shopping, are easier. Since muscles produce energy, having more muscle makes you feel more energetic. It also helps to keep you slim, because muscles raise the metabolic rate. This is the rate at which your body uses up energy.

Muscular fitness makes movement easier, which prevents injuries from accidents. Muscles also cushion our bones in a fall, and strengthen bones by pulling on them to make them move.

Anaerobic exercise tips

- Always work both muscles in each pair.
- Work all the major muscles in the body to make them balanced.
- Keep your joints in line and bend your knees not your back when lifting.

DID YOU KNOW?

Lactic acid

If our muscles hurt during exercise, it means a substance called lactic acid has built up. Lactic acid is produced in muscles when carbohydrate is burned for energy. When you stop, the acid disperses into the blood and you can continue exercising.

◀ Gymnasts need to be very flexible to perform many moves.

injuries while playing sport. It is also essential for gymnasts, ballet dancers and high-jumpers.

We can improve our flexibility by stretching. When we stretch, our muscles lengthen and relax. They become more elastic and allow our joints to move more fully.

It is very important to stretch before and after exercise. Stretching before exercise prepares our muscles for work, which helps prevent injury. Stretching after exercise helps our muscles recover by lengthening them after they have been contracted.

Stretching before and after exercise is important, but stretching at any time is good for you, especially after sitting or lying down. Try to stretch as soon as you get up in the morning and after sitting at your desk to prepare your muscles for movement.

Flexibility

Flexibility is the ability to move our joints fully. When we touch our toes, we are moving the joints in our spine. If we are flexible, we can touch our toes easily.

Being flexible makes it easier to do everyday tasks, such as reaching up to a shelf or picking something up from the floor. It can help prevent

Yoga

Yoga combines different stretches. Some are more difficult than others. Yoga improves flexibility as well as muscular strength and posture.

This woman is sitting in the lotus position in a yoga class. ▶

How can Exercise Help?

Taking exercise is good for our bodies and our minds.

Physical benefits of exercise

Exercise makes our bodies healthier in the following ways:

1. General fitness
We become fitter, we can keep doing physical activity for longer.

Downhill skiing requires motor fitness. ▼

2. Specific fitness
If we do a particular sport regularly, we will get better at it. For example, if we go swimming regularly, we will become better swimmers.

3. Motor fitness
Motor fitness is made up of agility, balance, co-ordination, power and reaction time. These skills improve naturally in sports that use them, or they can be improved with specific exercises.

▲ High jumping requires great flexibility as well as strength.

4. Immune system

Exercise strengthens the body's immune system. This is the group of cells and tissues that help defend the body against diseases. So exercise can help prevent disease.

5. Heart

Regular aerobic exercise makes the heart grow bigger. This means that more oxygen reaches the muscles in the heart. The heart rate slows down because it doesn't have to work as hard. This makes it less likely to have heart disease in later life. Fit people have lower heart rates than people who are unfit.

This cross-section of an artery shows the build up of cholesterol (in yellow). ▶

6. Blood system

Regular exercise reduces the amount of cholesterol, or fat, in your blood. This prevents cholesterol from building up in the arteries and making them narrower, which raises blood pressure. High blood pressure can lead to heart attacks.

Aerobic exercise also keeps the levels of sugar in blood stable. This protects against diabetes, a disease where the body cannot control its own levels of blood sugar.

7. Growth

Regular exercise helps the body grow in the healthiest way.

◀ A doctor measures a girl's height, to check she is still growing.

8. Body fat

Regular exercise helps control the amount of fat in our bodies because it burns fat to use as energy. Exercise also raises our metabolic rate for some hours after exercise, so we continue to burn fat even when we are at rest.

Food for exercise

The best foods to eat for exercise are natural carbohydrates such as potatoes, rice or pasta. These are stored in the muscles and are easily converted to energy. Avoid fatty foods such as crisps and chips, which are stored as body fat and only used for energy when the carbohydrates run out. Avoid sugary foods such as chocolate, too. They only give short bursts of energy and may make you feel more tired afterwards.

Burgers and chips are fatty foods that are hard for the body to convert to energy, and sugary drinks only give temporary bursts of energy. ▼

9. Posture

Exercise improves your posture, the way you hold your body, by making you more flexible and strong.

10. Lungs

Regular aerobic exercise strengthens the muscles in your lungs. Stronger lungs take deeper breaths, which means that fewer breaths are needed to take in the same amount of air. This means that the lungs don't have to work as hard. Lungs that breathe more easily are important for people with asthma.

11. Bones

Walking and running puts the weight of your body on your bones, which makes them more dense and strong. Lifting weights also strengthens your bones because muscles pull on them. Stronger bones are less likely to break when under pressure.

◀ A runner recovers after a cross-country race. Exercise makes your lungs work better and slows your normal breathing rate down.

This X-ray shows an arm with two broken bones. Exercise can stop bones breaking by making them more dense. ▶

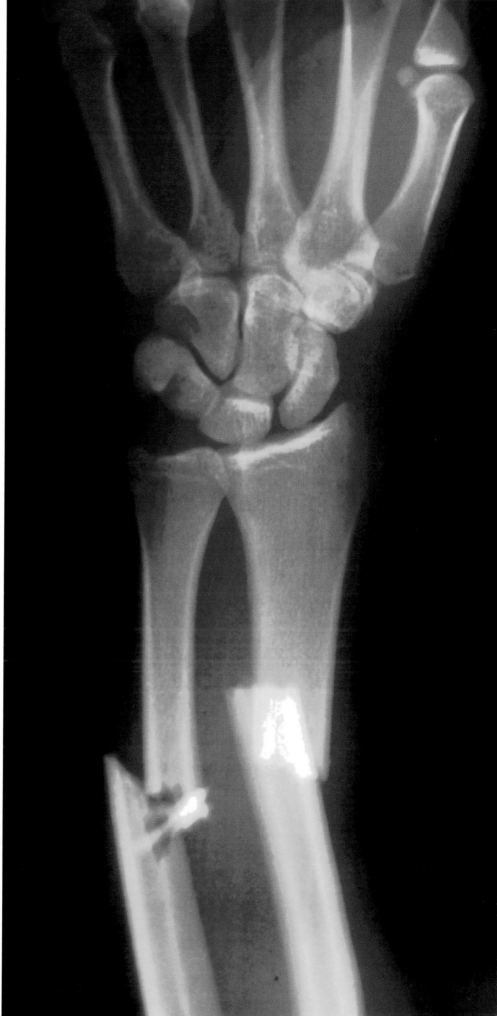

Bone density

It is important for girls to build up bone density when they are young to prevent brittle bones, or osteoporosis, when they are older. Osteoporosis is caused when bones become less dense, often when women are in their fifties and reach their menopause.

12. Digestion

Exercise speeds up the passage of food through the body, which prevents problems with digestion.

13. Skin

When we exercise we get hot. Our bodies sweat to lose heat and keep cool. Sweating keeps our pores clean, which makes our skin look its best.

14. Muscles

Aerobic exercise increases the amount of oxygen travelling to the muscles and the amount of energy that is produced. Weight lifting and other anaerobic exercise builds the muscles themselves. Having more muscle increases the metabolic rate, strength and energy levels. It also makes the body look more toned.

15. Sleep

People who exercise usually sleep better because they have used up excess energy.

Sit-ups make the stomach, or abdominal muscles, more toned and improve posture. ▼

16. Old age

Exercise keeps people healthy in old age and can help them live longer. Most people lose over half of their body's muscle between the ages of 30 and 70. This means that their metabolic rate slows down and it is easier to get fat. Taking exercise prevents people losing muscle, which stops them getting fat. Their muscle also keeps them strong and protects them from injury.

▲ Regular exercise protects the body against diseases in later life, such as heart disease and cancers.

True or false?

Muscle strengthening makes you bigger

This is true and false. Men have higher levels of a hormone called testosterone, which makes muscles bigger when they are trained. Women have low levels of testosterone, so if they do muscle-strengthening exercises, they do not grow much bigger. These exercises help women to stay slim.

Psychological benefits of exercise

Exercise helps our emotional and psychological health in the following ways:

1. Mood
Exercise cheers us up. This is because it increases the levels of endorphins in our blood. Endorphins are produced by the brain to relieve pain, and they make you feel good.

2. Stress
Exercise makes us less tense and stressed. This is because it reduces our blood pressure, heart rate and breathing rate, which makes us feel calmer. Exercise also helps the body get rid of two hormones that cause stress – adrenalin and noradrenalin.

3. Energy
Aerobic exercise gives us more energy for up to an hour afterwards. It also makes us more alert for all our waking hours.

The endorphins produced by exercise and the fun of playing sport make us feel good. ▼

▲ If you are worried about something, taking exercise may help you feel better.

4. Concentration

Exercise can improve our concentration because it makes us feel relaxed. It can help us to study and solve problems, as well as deal with everyday concerns.

5. Self-esteem and confidence

Regular exercise can raise our self-esteem because we see ourselves getting better at an activity. As our posture and figure improves, so does our confidence. People who exercise regularly have more confidence and self-esteem, which makes them less afraid to try new things and meet new people.

What is runner's high?

'Runner's high' is the extreme happiness felt by some people after exercising for over 20 minutes. It is caused by extra endorphins released into the blood.

6. New friends

Sports clubs and exercise classes are great ways to make new friends.

7. Brain

Martial arts, tennis and other sports that require agility, co-ordination and concentration stimulate the brain as well as the body. People whose brains are stimulated regularly are more mentally alert, have better memory and powers of thought. The brain is stimulated by an increase in the amount of oxygenated blood that is pumped round the body during exercise. It is also stimulated by the challenge of each situation.

◄ Table tennis stimulates the brain by demanding coordination skills and quick reactions.

8. Fun

By making us feel good, giving us more energy, raising our self-esteem and self-confidence, exercise is fun. When you first start taking exercise, it might seem hard at first, but remember it gets easier. You will soon have more energy and be able to enjoy working your body.

Judo, karate and other martial arts help to increase concentration and co-ordination. ▼

Get more active

You can take more exercise in many different ways. Simply being more active in the things you do every day will make you fitter. Try walking to school instead of taking the bus, or go swimming with friends instead of going to the cinema. Could you practise some football skills instead of watching television?

You should try to be active for at least an hour every day. This could be all at once or spread out over the day. But be careful not to do one type of exercise too much. If you only work one set of muscles every time you exercise, it can be easy to injure them.

Going for a bike ride with friends can be so much fun that you might not notice you're actually taking exercise. ▼

Cross-training

The safest type of exercise is cross-training because it mixes activities that work on all areas of fitness. For example, running improves aerobic fitness, weight-lifting improves muscular fitness and yoga works on flexibility. Try to do a bit of everything to get fit.

Volleyball improves the skills of motor fitness, such as co-ordination and balance, as well as working on general fitness. ▶

Warming up

At the start of any exercise, it's important to warm up and stretch. Warming up with gentle exercises gradually raises the heart and breathing rate, which means the heart isn't suddenly strained. Warming up also heats up the muscles, which makes them less likely to be injured.

Warming up and stretching helps prevent strained muscles and other injuries. ▼

How to warm up

- Do gentle exercises such as brisk walking, arm circling and knee bends.
- Stretch the muscles that will be used (see pages 32-33).

▲ Stretching after exercise is a good way to improve your flexibility.

Cooling down

At the end of exercise, cooling down gradually slows the activity down, so the heart doesn't have to work as hard. Stretching the muscles after exercise helps them recover. This is also a good time to work on flexibility.

How to cool down

- Do the same exercises to cool down as you did to warm up.
- Stretch the muscles that have been used (see pages 32-33). Hold them for up to 30 seconds.

Stretches

Try these stretches before and after exercise. It's a good idea to check with your PE teacher that you are doing them correctly.

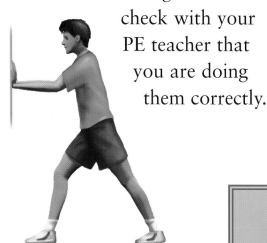

◄ **3. Back of leg (before exercise)**
Put one foot forward. Place your hands above the back knee, bend the back leg and lean forward.

4. Back of arms ▶
Stretch one arm above your head and reach your hand down your back. Gently press the elbow down with the other hand. Change arms and repeat.

▲ **1. Calf**
Push both hands against a wall, bend one leg and put the other straight back. Press the heel of the back leg into the ground. Change legs and repeat.

Back of leg

Do this stretch after exercise. Lying on your back, pull one knee towards your chest. Gently straighten the leg, holding it behind the calf. When the stretch feels less tight, gently pull the leg closer to your chest. Change legs and repeat.

▼ **5. Inside leg**
Sit with your legs apart and feet flexed. Reach both hands forwards towards your toes.

▲ **6. Shoulders**
Stretch one arm in front of you and across your chest. Gently pull the arm above the elbow joint towards the chest with the other hand. Change arms and repeat.

▲ **2. Front of thigh**
Hold one ankle behind your bottom, keeping your knees together and your hips forwards. Change legs and repeat.

▶ 7. Central and lower back

On all fours, pull your stomach in and round your back, dropping your chin down. Then raise your head and gently arch your back to reverse the stretch.

▲ 8. Upper back

Stretch both arms in front of you with your hands clasped and your head dropped.

▼ 10. Bottom

Lying on your back, rest your right ankle on your left knee and pull your left knee in towards your chest. Change sides and repeat.

▲ 12. Sides

Lying on your back with your knees bent, drop both knees to one side. Change sides and repeat.

▲ 9. Chest

Stretch both arms out behind you with your hands clasped. Raise your arms and hold.

▼ 11. Abdomen

Lie on your front and push up on your elbows with your chin up.

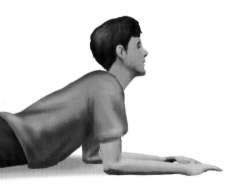

▲ 13. Spine

Stretch your arms above your head and reach as high as possible.

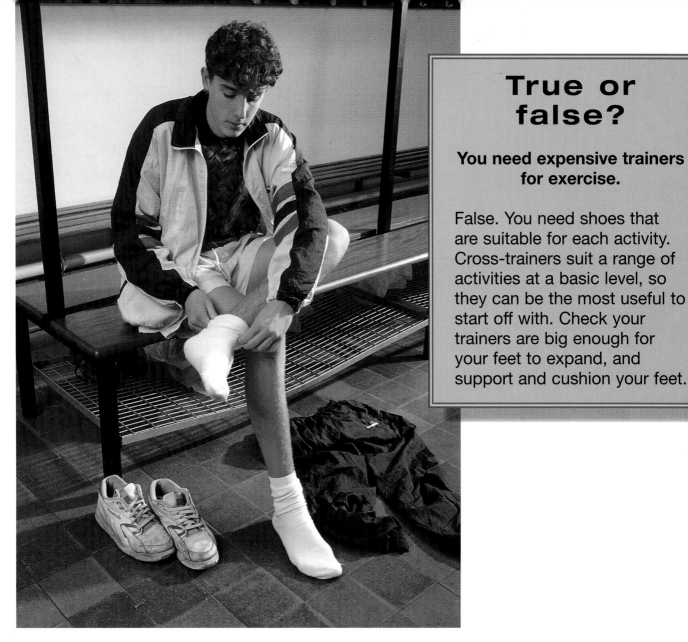

▲ Well-fitting trainers help prevent sprains and strains by cushioning and supporting the feet.

What to wear

Sports clothing is made using materials that draw sweat away from the body and dry quickly. But an old t-shirt and shorts or other light, loose-fitting clothing can be just as good, as long as it doesn't restrict your movements. Choose thick cotton to help absorb sweat, and girls may need a sports bra to prevent breast pain. Take an extra top to put on afterwards to stop you getting cold.

Hygiene and rest

Always shower after exercise and dry between your toes to prevent athlete's foot. This is a common foot disease among people who do sport. It can be caught from changing room floors, along with veruccas, so wear sandals when changing your shoes.

It's important to rest between exercise and to vary the type of exercise you do. Don't do the same type of aerobic exercise day after day, or you may strain a muscle or joint. If you get tired, slow down and stop.

This photograph shows the thin branches of the athlete's foot fungus magnified about 4,000 times. ▼

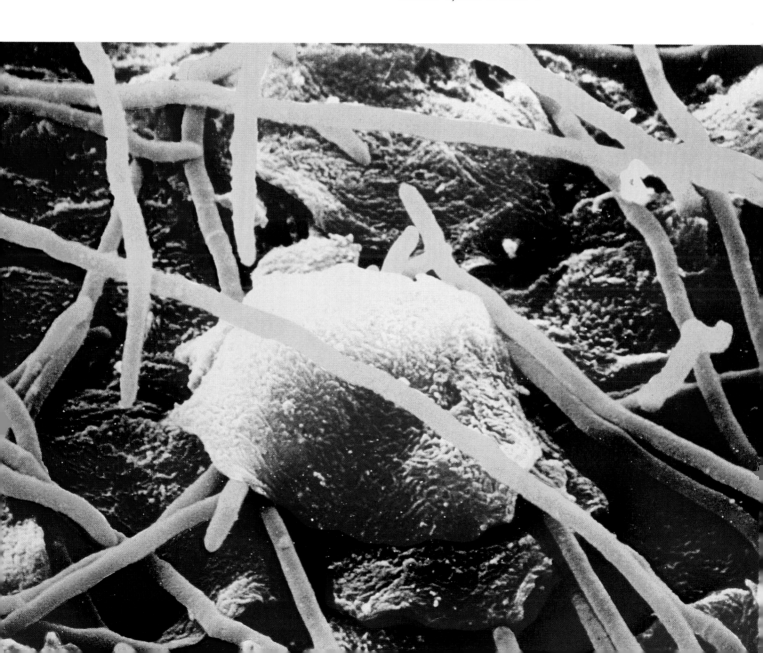

▲ Pasta is a useful form of carbohydrate for athletes that is easy and quick to cook.

What to eat

A healthy diet for exercise contains carbohydrates, protein, fruit and vegetables. Carbohydrates from rice and pasta are stored as glycogen and used as fuel during exercise. Protein from fish, meat, dairy foods and nuts helps to build muscle.

Carbohydrate loading

Many athletes prepare for events by encouraging their muscles to store more glycogen. They do this by eating more carbohydrates in the week before the event and training less.

Avoid sugary foods, which raise the blood-sugar levels and make the body produce insulin to bring them down again. After an initial energy boost, you feel more tired afterwards.

Diet tips

- Olive oil is a healthier type of fat than butter.
- Sweets and sugary foods contain fat and little nutrition.
- Snack on fruit instead of sweets.

When to eat and drink

After a large meal, wait at least two hours before exercising to give your body time to digest and avoid getting muscle cramp. For extra energy, carbohydrate snacks such as dried fruit are the quickest to turn into energy.

We lose a lot of fluid when we exercise through sweat. This can make us dehydrated, which puts a strain on our heart and other organs. So it's important to drink lots of water before and after exercise.

Athletes that take part in endurance events such as cycling or marathon running must drink while racing to avoid dehydration. ▶

Which Activity?

There are so many activities to choose from, it can be hard to decide which you will enjoy the most. It might help to decide at first whether you prefer a solo sport, such as running, or a group activity, such as a team game, combat or racket sport.

Snowboarding is a popular solo sport. ▼

Solo sports

Choose a solo sport if you prefer to set your own goals, organise yourself and prefer exercising alone. Look at the benefits and risks of each sport in the table opposite so you can choose one that suits you.

Clubs and classes

Joining a sports club is a good way of getting started in a solo sport as well as meeting other people. Fitness classes set to music, such as aerobics, step and circuit-training, are another fun way of getting fit. They are specially designed to combine aerobic and muscular training as well as flexibility.

◀ Tuition from a coach or trainer will help you improve much faster than on your own.

Solo sports

ACTIVITY	BENEFITS	RISKS
Walking	Fat-burning, aerobic fitness, leg strength	Accidental injuries
Running	Fat-burning, aerobic fitness, leg strength	Foot, leg and back problems
Swimming	Fat-burning, aerobic fitness, all-over strength, low joint stress	Shoulder injuries, no bone strengthening
Cycling	Fat-burning, aerobic fitness, leg strength	Knee and back problems; accidental injuries
Rowing/ canoeing/ kayaking	Fat-burning, aerobic fitness, upper body strength	Back and shoulder problems; drowning
Athletics	Power and leg strength	Leg and groin injuries
Gymnastics	Bone-building, balance, strength, flexibility, power	Joint damage, accidental injuries
Climbing	Strength and agility	Accidental injuries and natural hazards
Skiing	Leg strength, agility, balance, reflexes	Accidental injuries and natural hazards
Skating	Fat-burning, aerobic fitness, leg strength, balance	Leg and groin injuries, accidental injuries
Yoga	Flexibility, strength, balance	None
Weightlifting	Strength, muscle endurance	Muscle injuries

Group activities

Choose a group activity if you like competing against other people. In team games like football, you have to work for the good of the team, not yourself. Racket sports like tennis require agility and co-ordination. Combat sports like fencing improve mental discipline.

▲ In fencing, players score points by striking parts of their opponent's body with a sword's tip.

◀ In American football, players wear thick protective clothing as they hurl themselves into the other team.

DID YOU KNOW?

Calories

Calories are measurements of energy that the body makes from food. Some sports burn more calories than others. Running and cross-country skiing burn more calories than sports like climbing or karate.

Group activities

ACTIVITY	BENEFITS	RISKS
RACKET SPORTS		
Tennis	Coordination, agility, reflexes, bone strength	Ball and shoulder injuries
Squash	Coordination, agility, reflexes, bone strength	Ball and ankle injuries
TEAM GAMES		
Football	Leg strength, speed, power, aerobic fitness, bone-building, agility	Contact, leg and groin injuries
Netball/basketball	Leg strength, speed, power, aerobic fitness, bone-building, agility	Contact, knee, ankle & shoulder injuries
Cricket	Co-ordination, power, bone-building	Ball and shoulder injuries
Hockey	Leg strength, speed, power, aerobic fitness, bone-building, agility	Stick and leg injuries
COMBAT SPORTS		
Boxing	Aerobic fitness, upper body strength, coordination, bone-building, power, agility	Serious contact injuries
Karate	Flexibility, strength, speed, power, agility, bone-building, self-defence, coordination, mental discipline	Serious accidental injuries

Avoiding Problems

It's impossible to avoid injuries from sport altogether, but there are certain things you can do to help prevent them:

Clothing and equipment

Make sure that you have proper fitting shoes, and any equipment, for example the length of your ski when you go skiing, is the right size for you. Check that you have proper fitting protective clothing such as helmets and padding such as knee protectors.

A roller-hockey goalkeeper wears a helmet and protective padding. ▼

Over-training

▲ Well fitting, supportive trainers are essential for avoiding injury.

Injuries can happen when you haven't warmed up enough, or when you are tired. You get tired if you are not fit enough for an activity, or if you have simply done too much. Over-training puts stresses on your bones and muscles, which can lead to long-term problems. It can also weaken your immune system, so you catch colds more easily. Avoid over-training by varying the exercises you do, building them up gradually and taking lots of rest.

Exercise addiction

Exercise can become a problem if you get addicted to it. Exercise addicts only feel good when they are exercising and feel miserable if they are unable to. They may be addicted to the endorphins, or feel-good subtance that is produced by the body during exercise. Or it may be part of the psychological disease called anorexia, where sufferers want to lose as much weight as possible.

Body fat

We all need a certain amount of body fat to keep us warm and protect us from injury. Women need body fat for fertility, so they naturally have more fat than men. The ideal amount of body fat is 15 per cent for young men and 22 per cent for young women.

Many girls worry about their weight and have distorted images of their bodies, believing they are fatter than they really are. ▼

Adolescence

During adolescence, boys and girls have a period of growth when they grow suddenly in height. Girls have their growth spurt between the ages of 10 and 12, and boys between the ages of 12 and 17. If adolescents train hard during this growth spurt, their bones will not harden properly and may be weak in later life.

However, it is just as important to take exercise during adolescence to avoid getting fat.

Many adolescents feel self-conscious about their bodies and try to diet to lose weight, but most diets fail. Exercise is the best way to burn fat.

▲ Overweight parents often pass their unhealthy diets on to their children.

As you get fit, your body gets better at sweating. Fitter people sweat more than unfit people. ▼

Dehydration

When you exercise, you lose between 1–3 litres of sweat an hour. Avoid dehydration by drinking water before and after exercise. If your urine looks dark, you are a dehydrated and need to drink more water.

Glossary

adrenalin A hormone that is released by the body during exercise.

aerobic With oxygen. Aerobic exercise uses energy made from oxygen.

agility The ability to move quickly and easily.

anaerobic Without oxygen. Anaerobic exercise mainly uses energy not produced from oxygen.

atrium A chamber of the heart.

blood pressure The pressure of blood against the walls of the blood vessels.

brittle / dense bones Fragile bones that are easily broken.

carbohydrate Food substances such as starches and sugars that are made of carbon, hydrogen and oxygen.

carbon dioxide A gas that is in the air that we breathe out.

cholesterol A fatty substance found in the blood and tissues. High levels of cholesterol increase the risk of heart disease.

dehydrated Lacking water.

diabetes A disease in which the body is unable to produce insulin, which means it cannot absorb starches or sugars properly.

endorphins A substance produced by the brain to relieve pain.

endurance The ability to keep going at a task.

fertility The ability to produce young.

glycogen A carbohydrate stored in the liver and turned into glucose when the body needs energy.

lungs A pair of organs used to breathe. They pass oxygen to the blood and take out carbon dioxide.

menopause A stage in a woman's life when she becomes infertile.

noradrenaline A hormone produced during exercise that causes stress.

osteoporosis A disease in which the bones become brittle and easy to break. It often occurs in old people.

oxygen A gas found in the air that we use to breathe and make energy.

reflexes Responses.

stimulated Excited into action.

ventricle A chamber in the heart.

Finding Out More

Books to read

Health Choices: Exercise and Play by Cath Senker (Hodder Wayland, 2004)
Health Matters: Exercise and Your Health by Gillian Powell (Hodder Wayland, 2002)
It's Your Health!: Exercise by Beverley Goodger (Franklin Watts, 2004)
Just the Facts: Drugs and Sport by Clive Gifford (Heinemann, 2004)
Keeping Healthy: Exercise by Carol Ballard (Hodder Wayland, 2004)
Look After Yourself: Get some exercise! by Angela Royston (Heinemann, 2003)
What's at Issue?: Health and You by Bridget Lawless (Heinemann, 2000)

Organisations

The best place to find out about exercise is your local sports centre, swimming pool or ice rink. Private health clubs also run classes. Local libraries, newsagents and health food shops often have details about exercise classes and other activities taking place near you.

Your local council publish lists of organised holiday activities and sport taster sessions. Sport England is a useful point of contact for information about activities in your area.

Your school's lunchtime and after-school clubs are a good place to start a new sport. Your PE teachers will have a great deal of knowledge about sport and will be happy to point you in the right direction if you ask for help or information too!

www.wiredforhealth.org.uk provides useful information on leading healthy lifestyles for young people.

Health Development Agency
Holborn Gate
330 High Holborn
London WC1V 7BA
Tel: 020 7430 0850

FitKid UK
PO Box 5473
Poole
Dorset
BH17 9ZQ
Tel: 01202 775416

YMCA
640 Forest Road
London
E17 3DZ

Index